Forgiveness

Other Words by Pope John Paul II

Fear Not
(edited by Alexandria Hatcher)

A Pilgrim Pope
(edited by Cardinal Achille Silvestrini
with the assitance of Jerome M. Vereb, C.P.)

Forgiveness

Thoughts for the New Millennium

POPE JOHN PAUL II

EDITED BY ALEXANDRIA HATCHER

A Giniger Book

**Andrews McMeel
Publishing**

Kansas City

Forgiveness copyright © 1999 by The K.S. Giniger Company, Inc. All rights reserved. Printed in the U.S.A. No part of this book may be used or reproduced in any manner whatsoever without written permission except in the case of reprints in the context of reviews. For information, write Andrews McMeel Publishing, an Andrews McMeel Universal company, 4520 Main Street, Kansas City, Missouri 64111.

www.andrewsmcmeel.com

99 00 01 02 03 RDC 10 9 8 7 6 5 4 3 2 1

Library of Congress Cataloging-in-Publication Data on file.

ISBN: 0-7407-0498-2

Book design by Holly Camerlinck

Contents

Introduction   vii

Opening Prayer   xii

Theme: Sin   1

Interlude—The Son   27

Theme: Mercy   36

Interlude—The Holy Spirit   62

Theme: Penance (Conversion)   71

Interlude—The Father   97

Theme: Reconciliation (Salvation)   106

Introduction

Pope John Paul II understands forgiveness not as an abstract entity to talk about, but rather as a process to be lived. It is a process of conversion, and it is ongoing. The process begins with a consciousness of sin, followed by the recognition that God's love surpasses all sin, always. After we turn toward God's love and mercy, atonement, or penance, affords a means to begin anew, leading to our reconciliation with God, with our communities, with each other, and with ourselves.

In speaking of forgiveness, then, the Holy Father is speaking at the same time of conversion and, ultimately, of salvation itself. This means that the Trinitarian Mystery, long invoked by this Pope in all serious matters, is apparent in this process.

The unity of the Godhead, the most perfect communio personarum: *the unity of the Father and the Word in the uncreated gift, remains divinely transcendent.*

At the same time it becomes the ultimate dimension in the affairs of men and the world; and thanks to the Son having made all things subject to the Father in the Holy Spirit, the world once again plays its full part in the mystery of God, because God will be "all in all."

The Holy Father speaks of a "shattered world," reflecting divisions between individuals and groups and among nations. These divisions include violence, terrorism, torture, and oppression. The source of all divisions among us he sees as a "wound in man's innermost self. . . . In the light of faith we call it sin." We can "build a world without God," says John Paul, but "it is the reality of God that reveals and illustrates the mystery of man." He laments the loss of what he terms "a sense of sin."

And yet, he reminds us that where there is sin, there is always the possibility of God's forgiveness. Such is the transforming acceptance of the unconditional mercy of God through Jesus Christ, and our subsequent extending of that experience to other persons by accepting them. This is central to the Christian identity in the Lord's Prayer.

It is the "Our Father" that shows that divine forgiveness parallels the forgiveness that we give to those offending us. What was broken—the personal bond of covenant—separates us until true repentance and interior submission to God reestablishes this personal relationship.

When we link penance to the "metanoia" (conversion) of the Synoptic Gospels, it means the inmost change of heart and is closely connected to reconciliation. The Holy Father calls it appropriate—and very significant—to do this at the beginning of a new millennium, highlighting the spirit of penance, conversion, and reconciliation.

"That reconciliation is a fundamental driving force," he insists, "is reflected by our irrepressible desire for peace. This reconciliation is at least as profound as our divisions—and can be effected only by reaching—in order to heal—that original wound at the root of all other wounds."

John Paul follows his predecessors John XXIII and Paul VI in inviting to reconciliation the whole of humanity. He follows them further in his desire, already manifested on several occasions, to perform concrete acts of forgiveness himself on behalf of the historical Church. He states:

Acknowledging the weaknesses of the past is an act of honesty and courage which helps us to strengthen our faith, which alerts us to face today's temptations and challenges, and prepares us to meet them.

To that end, he invites us to respond to his call for the examination of conscience at the end of this millennium.

Here, then, we follow the Pope's process of forgiveness by devoting entire sections to sin, mercy, penance (conversion), and reconciliation (salvation). We acknowledge John Paul's Trinitarian sense of forgiveness by interspersing brief interludes on the Son, who bridges our humanness to God's mercy; on the Holy Spirit, who guides us toward atonement; and on the Father, in whom we seek the wholeness that reconciliation offers.

ALEXANDRIA HATCHER

May Christ's followers show forth their love
for the poor and the oppressed;
may they be one with those in need
and abound in works of mercy;
may they be compassionate toward all,
that they themselves may obtain indulgence
and forgiveness from you.

—FROM THE PRAYER OF HIS HOLINESS POPE JOHN PAUL II
FOR THE GREAT JUBILEE OF THE YEAR 2000

Sin

"*I have not come to invite the self-righteous to a change of heart, but sinners.*"

LUKE 5:32

$\mathcal{T}$he joy of every Jubilee is above all a joy based upon the forgiveness of sins, the joy of conversion . . . which is the precondition for reconciliation with God on the part of both individuals and communities.

$\mathcal{M}$an remains shut to God so long as the words
"Father, I have sinned against you"
are absent from his lips, above all while they are
absent from his conscience, from his "heart."

*T*emptation is nothing else but directing toward evil everything which man can and ought [to] put to good use.

$\mathcal{S}$ince all the faithful are in solidarity in the Christian community, there can never be a sin which does not have an effect on the whole community.

The forgiveness of sins first experienced in baptism
is a recurring need in the life of every Christian.
Restoring a proper sense of sin is the first step
to be taken in facing squarely the grave spiritual crisis
looming over men and women today,
a crisis which can well be described
as "an eclipse of conscience."

As a personal act, sin has its first and most
important consequences in the sinner himself:
that is, his relationship with God,
who is the very foundation of human life;
and also in his spirit, weakening his will
and clouding his intellect.

There is nothing so personal and untransferable in each individual as merit for virtue or responsibility for sin.

$\mathcal{I}$t is a truth of faith, also confirmed by our experience and reason, that the human person is free. This truth cannot be disregarded in order to place the blame for individuals' sins on external factors such as structures, systems, or other people.

Sin, in the proper sense, is always a personal act,
since it is an act of freedom
on the part of an individual person.

The demands of truth and love . . . presuppose
a frank recognition of the facts, together with a
readiness to forgive and to make amends
for our respective mistakes.

There is no sin, not even the most intimate and secret one, the most strictly individual one, that exclusively concerns the person committing it.

$\mathcal{S}$in is a product of man's freedom. But deep within its human reality there are factors at work which place it beyond the merely human, in the border area where man's conscience, will, and sensitivity are in contact with the dark forces which, according to Saint Paul, are active in the world almost to the point of ruling it.

As a rupture with God, sin is an act of disobedience by a creature who rejects, at least implicitly, the very one from whom he came and who sustains him in life. It is therefore a suicidal act.

$\mathcal{R}$ejection of God, rejection of his grace, and therefore opposition to the very source of salvation—these are manifestations whereby a person seems to exclude himself voluntarily from the path of forgiveness.

According to the Babel story, the result of sin is
the shattering of the human family,
already begun with the first sin and now reaching
its most extreme form on the social level.

$\mathcal{I}$t [sin] is the disobedience of a person who,
by a free act, does not acknowledge God's sovereignty
over his or her life, at least at that particular moment
in which he or she transgresses God's law.

*I*n the words of Saint John the Apostle,
"If we say we have no sin, we deceive ourselves,
and the truth is not in us. If we confess our sins,
he is faithful and just, and will forgive our sins." . . .
These words present the question of sin
in its human dimension.

Exclusion of God, rupture with God, disobedience to God: throughout the history of mankind this has been and is, in various forms, sin.

$\mathcal{W}$e shall have to evaluate the consequences of sin with eyes enlightened by faith. These consequences of sin are the reasons for division and rupture, not only within each person but also within the various circles of a person's life: in relation to the family, to the professional, and the social environment, as can often be seen from experience.

$\mathcal{T}$o acknowledge one's sin—to recognize oneself as being a sinner, capable of sin and inclined to commit sin—is the essential first step in returning to God.

$\mathcal{W}$e should always forgive, remembering that
we too are in need of forgiveness.

$\mathcal{G}$od is faithful to his eternal plan even when man, under the impulse of the Evil One and carried away by his own pride, abuses the freedom given to him.

$\mathcal{G}$od is faithful even when man,
instead of responding with love to God's love,
opposes him and treats him like a rival,
deluding himself and relying on his own power,
with the resulting break of relationship
with the one who created him.

24

Contemporary man experiences the threat of spiritual unfeelingness and even death of the conscience. This death is something deeper than sin: it is a slaying of the sense of sin.

$\mathcal{P}$roperly understood, justice constitutes the goal of forgiveness. In no passage of the Gospel message does forgiveness, or mercy as its source, mean indulgence toward evil, toward scandals, toward injury or insult.

The Son

To speak of reconciliation and penance is . . . an invitation
to rediscover . . . the very words with which our Savior
and Teacher Jesus Christ began his preaching:
"Repent, and believe in the gospel."

MARK 1:15

*J*esus himself puts the following significant words on the lips and in the heart of the prodigal son: "Father, I have sinned against heaven and before you."

*T*wo gestures are characteristic of Jesus' mission: healing and forgiving. Jesus' many healings clearly show his great compassion in the face of human distress . . . and that his mission, from the very beginning, is meant to free people from these evils.

$\mathcal{B}$y conquering through his death on the cross evil and the power of sin, by his loving obedience he brought salvation to all and became "reconciliation" for all. In him God reconciled man to himself.

*T*he Christian has within himself the presence
of Christ and the mystery of Christ,
which is the mystery of God's loving-kindness.

$\mathcal{W}$e can . . . relate all our reflections on the whole mission of Christ to his mission as the one who reconciles.

In Jesus' eyes, healings are also a sign of spiritual salvation, namely liberation from sin. By performing acts of healing, he invites people to faith, conversion, and the desire for forgiveness.

$\mathcal{R}$econciliation is a gift of God, an initiative on his part. But our faith teaches us that this initiative takes concrete form in the mystery of Christ the Redeemer, the reconciler and the liberator of man from sin in all its forms.

Christ came not to condemn but to forgive,
to show mercy. And the greatest mercy of all is found
in his being in our midst and calling us to meet him
and to confess with Peter that he is
"the Son of the living God."

Mercy

"Blessed are the merciful, for they shall obtain mercy."

MATTHEW 5:7

$\mathcal{I}$nfinite are the readiness and power of forgiveness which flow continually from the marvelous value of the sacrifice of the Son. No human sin can prevail over this power or even limit it.

Courage, dearest brothers and sisters. The world is thirsty, even without knowing it, for the divine mercy, and you are called to proffer this prodigious water, healing to soul and body.

$\mathcal{M}$an has a deep need to meet with the mercy of God, today more than ever. To feel himself radically understood, in the weakness of his wounded nature, above all to have spiritual experience of that love which receives, enlivens, and resuscitates to new life.

$\mathcal{I}$t [repentance] is the act of the prodigal son who returns to his father and is welcomed by him with the kiss of peace. It is an act of honesty and courage. It is an act of entrusting oneself, beyond sin, to the mercy that forgives.

No human sin can erase the mercy of God,
or prevent him from unleashing all his
triumphant power, if we only call upon him.

The person is a being for whom the only suitable dimension is love. We are just to a person if we love him. This is as true for God as it is for man. Love for a person excludes the possibility of treating him as an object of pleasure. . . . Love . . . requires the affirmation of the person as a person.

*L*et us have recourse to God through Christ, mindful of the words of Mary's Magnificat, which proclaim mercy "from generation to generation." Let us implore God's mercy for the present generation.

$\mathcal{T}$he mystery of Christ . . . obliges me to proclaim
mercy as God's merciful love, revealed in that same
mystery of Christ. It likewise obliges me to have
recourse to that mercy and to beg for it
at this difficult, critical phase of the history of the
Church and of the world.

$\mathcal{W}$e are to proclaim and to introduce into life the mystery of mercy, supremely revealed in Jesus Christ. . . . This mystery is the source of a life different from the life which can be built by man. . . . It is precisely in the name of this mystery that Christ teaches us to forgive always.

In the whole of this messianic program of Christ, in the whole revelation of mercy through the cross, could man's dignity be more highly respected and ennobled, for, in obtaining mercy, he is in a sense the one who at the same time shows mercy.

Mercy in itself, as a perfection of the infinite God, is also infinite. Also infinite therefore, and inexhaustible, is the Father's readiness to receive the prodigal children who return to his home.

Conversion to God always consists in discovering
his mercy, that is, in discovering that love
which is patient and kind
as only the Creator and Father can be . . .

$\mathcal{M}$an attains to the merciful love of God,
his mercy, to the extent that he himself is
interiorly transformed in the spirit of that love
toward his neighbor.

*I*n its human dimension, sin is countered
by the truth of divine love, which is just, generous,
and faithful, and which reveals itself
above all in forgiveness and redemption.

The parable of the prodigal son shows that . . . the relationship of mercy is based on the common experience of that good which is man, on the common experience of the dignity that is proper to him.

$\mathcal{M}$ercy is an indispensable dimension of love; it is, as it were, love's second name and, at the same time, the specific manner in which love is revealed.

The genuine face of mercy has to be ever revealed anew. In spite of many prejudices, mercy seems particularly necessary for our times.

$\mathcal{M}$ercy . . . has the power to confer on justice
a new content, which is expressed
most simply and fully in forgiveness.

$\mathcal{T}$he parable of the prodigal son expresses in a simple but profound way the reality of conversion. Conversion is the most concrete expression of the working of love and of the presence of mercy in the human world.

*I*n the preaching of the prophets, *mercy* signifies
a special power of love, which prevails over
the sin and infidelity of the chosen people.

*C*hrist addressed himself to people who not only knew the concept of mercy, but who also, as the people of God of the Old Covenant, had drawn from their age-long history a special experience of the mercy of God. This experience was social and communal, as well as individual and interior.

*F*orgiveness shows that, over and above
the process of "compensation" and "truce"
specific to justice, love is necessary, so that man
may affirm himself as man.

$\mathcal{C}$hrist, in revealing the love-mercy of God, at the same time demanded from people that they also should be guided in their lives by love and mercy.

On the basis of this way of manifesting
the presence of God who is Father, love, and mercy,
Jesus makes mercy one of the principal
themes of his preaching.

Christ emphasizes so insistently the need
to forgive others that, when Peter asked him how
many times he should forgive his neighbor,
he answered with the symbolic number of
"seventy times seven," meaning that he must be able
to forgive everyone every time.

The Holy Spirit

"I will ask the Father and he will give you another Paraclete [Advocate]—to be with you always: the Spirit of truth, whom the world cannot accept, since it neither sees him nor recognizes him. But you can recognize him because he remains with you and will be within you."

JOHN 14:16–17

Many factors work together today to kill
the consciences of people of our time.
This corresponds to what Christ called "the sin
against the Holy Spirit." Such sin begins
when the Word of the cross no longer speaks to man
as the last cry of love, with power to tear hearts.

No matter how many and great the obstacles put in his way by human frailty and sin, the Spirit, who renews the face of the earth, makes possible the miracle of the perfect accomplishment of the good.

God's mercy reaches its fullness in the gift
of the Spirit, who bestows new life
and demands that it be lived.

$\mathcal{I}$t is the Spirit who opens people's hearts
so that they can believe in Christ and "confess him."

The flowering of the gift of mercy offers liberation from the slavery of evil and gives the strength to sin no more. Through the gift of new life, Jesus makes us sharers in his love and leads us to the Father in the Spirit.

*U*nity must be the result of a true conversion
of everyone, the result of mutual forgiveness,
of theological dialogue and fraternal relations,
of prayer, and of complete docility to the action of
the Holy Spirit, who is also the *Spirit of Reconciliation*.

$\mathcal{I}$t is a task of learning the weaknesses and falls
of those faithful people, assessing their desire
for renewal and their efforts to achieve it, discerning
the action of the Holy Spirit in their hearts, imparting
to them a forgiveness which God alone can grant.

$\mathcal{S}$in at its worst is a reality that not only affects
a man's subjective conscience and will,
but also affects his relationship with God
the Holy Spirit, the fount of grace.

Penance
(Conversion)

"Have mercy on me, O God, in your goodness;
in the greatness of your compassion wipe out my offense."

PSALM 51:1

"Receive the Holy Spirit. If you forgive men's sins, they are
forgiven them; if you hold them bound, they are held bound."

JOHN 20:22–23

Nothing is more personal and intimate than this
Sacrament, in which the sinner stands alone
before God with his sin, repentance, and trust.
No one else can repent in his place
or ask forgiveness in his name.

If it is true that sin in a certain sense shuts man off from God, it is likewise true that remorse for sins opens up all the greatness and majesty of God, his Fatherhood above all, to man's conscience.

$\mathcal{R}$eparation for evil and scandal,
compensation for injury, and satisfaction for insult
are conditions for forgiveness.

Constant reception of the Sacraments,
those of Reconciliation and the Eucharist in particular,
cleanse and enrich us with the grace of Christ
and make us "new," in accordance
with Jesus' pressing call: "Be converted."

$\mathcal{R}$ecourse to the Sacrament [of Penance] is necessary when even only one mortal sin has been committed. However, the Christian who believes in the effectiveness of sacramental forgiveness has recourse to the Sacrament with a certain frequency, even when it is not a case of necessity.

$\mathcal{I}$t is one's whole existence that becomes penitential, that is to say, directed toward a continuous striving for what is better.

Penance means changing one's life in harmony
with [a] change of heart.

$\mathcal{G}$ive yourselves over with humility and trust
to repentance. The Father of mercies is ready
to give you his forgiveness and his peace
in the Sacrament of Reconciliation.

*P*enance is a conversion that passes from the heart to deeds, and then to the Christian's whole life.

*T*he *sign of forgiveness*, conferred through the Sacrament of Penance . . . is . . . as a gift of his goodness and loving-kindness to be offered to all—a special Sacrament for the forgiveness of sins committed after baptism.

$\mathcal{T}$he work of conversion is performed in . . .
interior intimacy with God. Words resound in that
interior privacy and intimacy with God himself,
in all the truth of one's own heart and conscience.

We mature spiritually by converting to God, and conversion is effected through prayer as well as through fasting and almsgiving, properly understood.

*P*enance, conversion: this is the path,
not a sad but a liberating path.
Metanoeite—Be converted.

Only faith can give us certainty that at that moment
every sin is forgiven and blotted out
by the mysterious intervention of the Savior.

*C*onversion is actually nothing less than a return to God, through evaluating earthly realities in the unfailing light of his truth. This evaluation leads us to ever clearer consciousness of . . . [our] transit through the wearisome affairs of this earth.

*S*ynonymous with conversion is also the word *penitence* . . . penitence as medicine, reparation, as *change of mentality* . . . penitence as the expression of a free and joyous commitment to follow Christ.

$\mathcal{M}$an has to face up sadly to what he has lost, what he has deprived himself of by committing sin, living in sin; so that that decisive step may ripen in him: "I will break away and return to my Father." He must once more see the face of that Father upon whom he had turned his back.

Conversion is a particularly profound inward act in [the doing of] which the individual cannot be replaced by others and cannot make the community be a substitute for him.

$\mathcal{B}$y holding fast to Christ the Redeemer of man, one undertakes a journey of authentic conversion. This includes both a negative aspect, that of liberation from sin, and a positive aspect, that of choosing good, accepting the ethical values expressed in the natural law, which is confirmed and deepened by the gospel.

The call to conversion as the indispensable condition of Christian love is particularly important in contemporary society, where the very foundations of an ethically correct vision of human existence often seem to have been lost.

$\mathcal{W}$e cannot preach conversion
unless we ourselves are converted anew each day.

The Letter to the Hebrews speaks of being made perfect through suffering. . . . The purifying flames of trial and sorrow have the power to transform us from within by unleashing our love, teaching us compassion for others, and thus drawing us closer to Christ.

At the end of this second millennium
we must make an examination of conscience:
where we are, where Christ has brought us,
where we have deviated from the gospel.

To obtain forgiveness one must implore, becoming part of the loud cries of Christ the Redeemer. Through all of this one must proclaim glory. Prayer is always an *opus gloriae* (a work, a labor, of glory).

Doing penance, in the fullest sense of the term, [means] repenting, showing this repentance, adopting a real attitude of repentance—which is the attitude of the person who starts out on the road of return to the Father.

The Father

"I do not pray for them alone.
I pray also for those who will believe in me
through their word
that all may be one as you,
Father, are in me, and I in you;
I pray that they may be [one] in us
that the world may believe that you sent me. . . .
I living in them, you living in me
that their unity may be complete."

JOHN 17:20, 21, 23A

$\mathcal{T}$he whole of the Christian life is like a great pilgrimage to the house of the Father, whose unconditional love for every human creature, and in particular for the "prodigal son," we discover anew each day. This pilgrimage takes place in the heart of each person, extends to the believing community, and then reaches to the whole of humanity.

The tragic consequence of rejecting the Father
becomes evident in man's inner disorder
and in the breakdown of harmony between
man and woman, brother and brother.

$\mathcal{R}$efusal of God's fatherly love
and of his loving gifts is always at the root
of humanity's divisions.

The parable of the prodigal son is above all the story of the inexpressible love of a Father—God—who offers to his son when he comes back to him the gift of full reconciliation.

*T*he story of the prodigal son reminds us
of the need for a profound transformation of hearts
through the rediscovery of the Father's mercy,
and through victory over misunderstanding and
over hostility among brothers and sisters.

$\mathcal{R}$econciliation is principally a gift
of the Heavenly Father.

This prodigal son is man—every human being bewitched by the temptation to separate himself from his Father to lead his own independent existence.

$\mathscr{I}$t is especially for these last [the poor, the blind, the broken, sinners] that the Messiah becomes a particularly clear sign of God who is love, a sign of the Father. In this visible sign the people of our own time, just like the people then, can see the Father.

Reconciliation
(Salvation)

*This means that if anyone is in Christ, he is a new creation.
The old order has passed away; now all is new! All this has been done
by God, who has reconciled us to himself through Christ and has given
us the ministry of reconciliation. I mean that God, in Christ, was reconciling the world to himself, not counting men's transgressions against
them, and that he has entrusted the message of reconciliation to us.
This makes us ambassadors for Christ, God as it were appealing
through us. We implore you, in Christ's name: be reconciled to God!"*

2 CORINTHIANS 5:17–20

Conversion to God is always the fruit of the "rediscovery" of this Father, who is rich in mercy.

The work of reconciliation, the path toward unity, may be long and difficult. But, as on the road to Emmaus, the Lord himself is with us on the way. . . . He will be with us until the much-awaited moment comes when we shall be able to rejoice together in acknowledgement of him in the Sacred Scriptures and in "the breaking of the bread."

*R*econciliation with God is also reconciliation . . . in a certain sense with all of creation, whose harmony is violated by sin.

he fact that the good news of reconciliation is preached by Christians who are divided among themselves weakens their witness. It is thus urgent to work for the unity of Christians. . . . Efforts toward unity are themselves a sign of the work of reconciliation which God is bringing about in our midst.

We need to be forgiven much more often than we need to forgive.

*T*here can be no conversion without the
acknowledgement of one's own sin. . . .
The message and ministry of penance
are addressed to all men and women,
because all need conversion and reconciliation.

$\mathcal{T}$o become reconciled with God presupposes and includes detaching oneself consciously and with determination from the sin into which one has fallen.

*P*ersonal conversion is the necessary
path for harmony between individuals.

The Church, if she is to be *reconciling*, must
begin by being a *reconciled Church* . . . united
in the commitment to be continually converted
to the Lord and to live as new people
in the spirit and practice of reconciliation.

$\mathcal{T}$he Church's reconciling role must therefore be carried out in accordance with that intimate link which closely connects the forgiveness and remission of the sin of each person with the fundamental and full reconciliation of humanity that took place with the redemption.

*N*either reconciliation nor unity is possible outside or in opposition to the truth.

The paths [for reconciliation] are precisely those of conversion of heart and victory over sin, whether this latter is selfishness or injustice, arrogance or exploitation of others, attachment to material goods or the unrestrained quest for pleasure.

The chosen people, and each of its members,
will find, every time that they have sinned,
the strength and the motive for turning to the Lord
to remind him of what he had exactly revealed
about himself and to beseech his forgiveness.

The means [of reconciliation] are those of faithful and loving attention to God's word; personal and community prayer; and in particular the Sacraments, true signs and instruments of reconciliation.

Reconciliation between people is and
can only be the fruit of the redemptive act of Christ,
who died and rose again to conquer the kingdom
of sin, to reestablish the covenant with God
and thus break down the dividing wall
which sin had raised up between people.

We speak about the reconciliation of the whole human family and the conversion of the heart of every individual, of his or her return to God, . . . because . . . there can be no union among people without an internal change in each individual.

The longing for reconciliation, and reconciliation itself, will be complete and effective only to the extent that they reach—in order to heal it—that original wound which is the root of all other wounds: namely, sin.

$\mathcal{S}$ome consider reconciliation as an impossible
dream which ideally might become the lever
for a true transformation of society. For others,
it is to be gained by arduous efforts and
therefore a goal to be reached
through serious reflection and action.

God's salvation is the work of a love greater than man's sin. Love alone can wipe out sin and liberate from sin. Love alone can consolidate man in the good, in the unalterable and eternal good.

$\mathcal{T}$he primacy and superiority of love vis-à-vis justice—this is a mark of the whole of revelation—are *revealed precisely through mercy.* This seemed so obvious to the psalmists and prophets that the very term *justice* ended up meaning the salvation accomplished by the Lord and his mercy.

$\mathcal{G}$od does not close his heart to any of his children.
He waits for them, looks for them,
goes to meet them at the place where
the refusal of communion imprisons them
in isolation and division. He calls them to gather
about his Table in the joy of the feast
of forgiveness and reconciliation.

$\mathcal{T}$he most precious result of the forgiveness obtained
in the Sacrament of Penance consists
in reconciliation with God. . . . This reconciliation
with God leads . . . to other reconciliations,
which repair the breaches caused by sin.

*T*he forgiven penitent is reconciled with himself in his inmost being, where he regains his own true identity. He is reconciled with his brethren whom he has in some way attacked and wounded.

He is reconciled with the Church.

He is reconciled with all creation.

$\mathcal{R}$edemption is always greater than man's sin and the "sin of the world." The power of the redemption is infinitely superior to the whole range of evil in man and the world.

He who forgives and he who is forgiving
encounter one another at an essential point,
namely, the dignity or essential value of the person,
a point which cannot be lost and the affirmation
of which, or its rediscovery,
is a source of the greatest joy.